MICHAEL GNAROWSKI is Professor of English at Carleton University.

When *New Provinces* first appeared in 1936, it represented four years of planning, argument, and compromise, and an additional two and a half years of correspondence and editorial preparation. This prolonged effort was brought to a successful end with the publication of a slim collection of verse, the work of six writers, Robert Finch, Leo Kennedy, A.M. Klein, E.J. Pratt, F.R. Scott, and A.J.M. Smith.

At the time it was published it received little critical attention and had even less popular appeal; after nearly a year the book had sold only 82 copies, 10 of them to one of the contributors. Only E.K. Brown, writing for *University of Toronto Quarterly* in 1937, seemed to realize that *New Provinces* 'marked the emergence ... of a group of poets who may well have a vivifying effect on Canadian poetry.'

Since that time this small volume has been recognized as a monument in Canadian literature, a singular event in a literary process which stemmed from the origins of Canadian modernism and its beginnings in Montreal, marking the first collective effort to introduce poets who came to represent the new establishment.

Michael Gnarowski's introduction tells the fascinating story of the genesis of the idea for the book and the difficulties that were encountered.

Literature of Canada

Poetry and Prose in Reprint

Douglas Lochhead, General Editor

New Provinces

Poems of Several Authors

Introduction by Michael Gnarowski

UNIVERSITY OF TORONTO PRESS
TORONTO AND BUFFALO

University of Toronto Press 1976
Toronto and Buffalo
Printed in Canada

Library of Congress Cataloging in Publication Data
Main entry under title:

New provinces.

(Literature of Canada)
Reprint of the 1936 ed. published by Macmillan, Toronto.
Bibliography: p.
1. Canadian poetry—20th century.
PR9195.7.N4   1976   821'.5'08   76-45350
ISBN 0-8020-2246-4
ISBN 0-8020-6299-7 pbk.

New Provinces: Poems of Several Authors was originally published in 1936
by the Macmillan Company of Canada Limited, Toronto.

This book has been published with the assistance of grants from the
Ontario Arts Council and the McLean Foundation.

Preface

Yes, there is a Canadian literature. It does exist. Part of the evidence to support these statements is presented in the form of reprints of the poetry and prose of the authors included in this series. Much of this literature has been long out of print. If the country's culture and traditions are to be sampled and measured, both in terms of past and present-day conditions, then the major works of both our well-known and our lesser-known writers should be available for all to buy and read. The Literature of Canada series aims to meet this need. It shares with its companion series, The Social History of Canada, the purpose of making the documents of the country's heritage accessible to an increasingly large national and international public, a public which is anxious to acquaint itself with Canadian literature — the writing itself — and also to become intimate with the times in which it grew.

DL

Introduction

When *New Provinces* finally appeared in May 1936, it represented four years of planning, argument, and compromise and two and a half years of actual correspondence and editorial preparation. This prolonged effort was brought to a successful end with the publication of a slim collection of verse bound in green cloth, the work of one older and five younger writers. It was offered as the new poetry of the time. Now, viewed in retrospect, the appearance of this entirely unpretentious anthology was a singular event in a literary process which stemmed from the origins of Canadian modernism and its beginnings in Montreal.

New Provinces reaches back a dozen years from its date of publication to a series of unusual events of the middle nineteen-twenties, events which centred on McGill University and a group of young writers there, among whom A.J.M. Smith was the recognized leader. Smith possessed a precocious sensibility and a sharp sense of critical awareness as far as contemporary poetry on the world scene was concerned. He initiated matters by prevailing upon the Students' Society to allow him to edit *The McGill Daily Literary Supplement* (1924-5), with Allan B. Latham as associate editor. The next step was *The McGill Fortnightly Review* (1925-7), a more substantial and ambitious publication in the format of a periodical, and in the more permanent pages of which the ideas of modernism had practice and significant play. It is in the pages of the *Fortnightly* that Smith got properly started on a long career of articles, prefaces, and critical commentary which, for the purposes of this discussion, would lead to his 'rejected' preface to *New Provinces*.

At the turn of the century, the poetry of Britain had struck Ezra Pound as 'a horrible agglomerate compost ... a doughy mess...'[1] A quarter of a century later, the matter of Canadian poetry was of like kind, and F.R. Scott would be moved to give sharp notice of this in 'The Canadian Authors Meet,' a much anthologized poem which has become a classic in its own right. The activity at McGill, then – almost too short-lived for its accomplishments – was aimed at countering the set and insipid ways of traditional verse, and at turning poetry in a definite and new direction. The group, consisting of A.J.M. Smith, A.P.R. Coulborn, F.R. Scott, A.B. Latham, Leon Edel, and the loosely attached Leo Kennedy ('I've just read again that I attended McGill. Wrong. I attended the U of Montreal.') was soon dispersed by the claims of jobs, careers, and post-graduate studies. But it had learned its lessons well, and some of these young writers reassembled soon after to help edit *The Canadian Mercury* (1928-9). All of this served as valuable experience and preparation for the next decade.

The nineteen-thirties opened with a terrible and vengeful suddenness. They meant the Depression with its sad record of social and economic dislocation; the cresting swell of various forms of fascist ideology; the powerful tug and pull of left-wing politics and allegiances; and, seemingly everywhere, intellectual *angst* and the bleak intimations of a renewed wasteland (Leavis: 'Everywhere ... a process of standardization, mass-production, and levelling-down goes forward...'[2]). The times hardly seemed right for new verse, or, for that matter, for collections and anthologies of it. But, the state of the world and the pessimism of Leavis notwithstanding, the thirties in Canada, scarred as they may have been, were also marked by a cautious enterprise and an edging towards new writing and new ideas in criticism. Leo Kennedy managed to publish *The Shrouding* in 1933. *The Canadian Forum*, which had had an established policy of encouraging new writers, also served as an outlet for a series of related, short articles — a first batch aimed at knocking the 'Confederation' poets out of the centre of the ring; a second, intended to focus attention on the emerging new poets. There was also a good deal of public debate and argument supplied by the poets themselves. It ranged from the exhortations of Smith's 'Wanted — Canadian Criticism' in the April 1928 issue of the *Forum*, to Scott's 'New Poems for Old: I — The Decline of Poesy'; and 'II — The Revival of Poetry' in the May and June 1931 issues of the same magazine. The *Forum* served as a platform for free and enlightened exchange, and although not primarily a literary periodical, it helped move Canadian writing towards a milestone in the year 1936, which saw the publication of W.E. Collin's *The White Savannahs* and of the present collection, *New Provinces.*

Internationally, 1936 was the high-water mark of a decade of particular significance and profound upset. Remembered for the challenge and drama of the Spanish Civil War, which had such an immense effect on writers everywhere, it was also a year which saw opinions polarized and men driven to take their stand. In William York Tindall's words, 'Franco's Spain provided from 1936 to 1938 the emotional centre.'[3] For Canadian poets, in particular for A.J.M. Smith and F.R. Scott, and for others of their generation, Livesay, Klein, and Kennedy, that span of the first half of the thirties which coincided with the planning and preparation of *New Provinces* became, as well, a period of soul-searching, of a growing sense of social responsibility and concrete political action. It was a time of considerable debate in British literary circles, the period of Auden and Spender; of C. Day Lewis and Christopher Caudwell, the latter to die in the war in Spain. It was also the period which produced the group manifesto, *A Hope for Poetry* (1934), and it witnessed the publication of two important anthologies of contemporary poetry edited by Michael Roberts: *New Signatures* in 1932 and *New Country* in 1933. Of all this activity both A.J.M. Smith and F.R. Scott were fully aware. They and their colleagues felt pressed by the structures of a bourgeois society patently in conflict within itself, rocked by a contest between the traditionally uncurbed rights of the individual on the one hand, and the needs and promise of social advance and experiment on the other. As Tindall put it so aptly of the British poets: 'Bourgeois by nature, proletarian by sympathy, they found themselves neither here nor there.'[4] The cryptic yet tentative tone of F.R. Scott's preface to *New Provinces*, and the confident, politically assertive tenor of Smith in his own rejected preface to the same collection are evidence of the range of debate and the fulness of the social dilemma.

Early in 1934, the task of assembling and examining material for a small anthology of representative Canadian verse was given quickened interest by the dispatch of letters by F.R. Scott to two key figures: A.J.M. Smith and E.J. Pratt. These letters spearheaded a correspondence of substantial volume and interest. As far as it bears on the making of *New Provinces*, the steady exchange of letters would last for two and a half years, and would involve Robert Finch as well as some likely and not-so-likely publisher-prospects for the anthology. From the outset Scott functioned as the co-ordinator, and his address as a clearing house for the editorial business of *New Provinces*. Kennedy – and

Klein, to a somewhat lesser extent — assisted in the editorial process in Montreal, especially Kennedy, who had a strong hand in the selection of poems and helped out with Scott's version of the preface.

The idea for a small anthology had originally arisen in conversations between F.R. Scott, A.J.M. Smith, and Leo Kennedy. On the suggestion of Smith (he later plumped strongly for the inclusion of Dorothy Livesay and W.W.E. Ross), the plan had been extended beyond the Montreal nucleus, so much so that by 2 January 1934 E.J. Pratt had become an important part of the scheme, and Scott was writing to ask him to invite Robert Finch into the project. In the same letter, a sense of collective responsibility is at least partially established with Scott saying: 'I would be glad to hear from you. ... and also in regard to the selections from Smith, Kennedy and myself which I left with you.' A short week later, Pratt replied enclosing Finch's contribution, and also talked about their 'group of six' which brought A.M. Klein firmly into the picture. There was much jockeying about of poems at this early stage. Material was put up for the anthology, then withdrawn for, presumably, better work. The mood was one of buoyancy and optimism for the prospects of the collection. In his letter to Pratt of 11 January 1934, Scott wrote:

> We are not aiming at anything extraordinarily experimental, but so far as possible we would like to indicate that we are all post-Eliot. I wish we could introduce a touch of political radicalism somewhere.

On 15 February 1934, it was Smith's turn to urge matters along towards an important proposal. In a letter both long and, at times, impatient, he asked Scott about the progress of the book; wanted to know which poems were being included and what the others thought of his — at times acerbic — comments; and, more significantly, raised the question of an introduction. He proceeded to outline his 'ideas' for it, spelling out the following major points:

a) Canadian poetry has been conscious of its position in space, but not in time.

b) This body of verse represents the emergence of a group of young Canadian poets who are aware of the new developments of their art in France, England and U.S.

c) Their technique elegant and appropriate — occasionally a rhetoric derived from the Elizabethans through Eliot. A mingling of the 'poetic' and the colloquial. Absence of fustian; overthrow of the 'poetic subject' and of 'poetic' language that has characterized Canadian poetry in the past.

d) As a conclusion — make a modest claim that this book represents something of importance in Canada, while at the same time admitting that in England and the U.S. (a bitter pill for the Canadian public) there is, of course a comparatively large body of contemporary writing of equal or superior merit.

e) It is significant that there is nothing national about the contents of this book.

The other 'ideas' pointed to the value of pure poetry, metaphysical poetry, political poetry, and satire. Smith also took the opportunity to advance the cause of Dorothy Livesay ('I wish we could get some verse that is definitely politically left wing and at the same time good poetry') and of W.W.E. Ross ('and if we could get those poems he had in *The Dial* we would be getting something of very definite value'). Scott responded to these suggestions on 17 February 1934 with approval and information:

> The anthology is well on the way, but has not yet been submitted to Macmillan's. I spent last weekend in Toronto, and had an evening with Finch and Pratt. On the strength of your extreme but none too severe criticism of Finch I more or less laid down the law as to what sort of verse we want from them. Finch took it very graciously but Pratt was a little taken aback at first, although he came around afterwards. 'Who is this man Smith?' he asked. I assured him that you were the real leader of the young movement and that your word was law. It seemed to cow him for a bit.
>
> As a result of the evening we pretty well settled on the material of Finch's and Pratt's, and they had a chance to look over our stuff. ... I like your idea of the Introduction immensely, and the subjects you suggest appeal to me as being important. I wish you would prepare a draft and submit it to us; you are obviously the person for the job. You will have to be careful not to make claims for a greater radicalism than this volume will show. I entirely agree with you that we should turn our poetical interest in the direction of politically left-wing verse, but I have a feeling that the publication of this anthology will do more to help us in that direction than anything else: we shall have got something out of our systems and will be freer to develop the tendencies that there are in the collection.

By 3 March 1934, the first draft of the anthology was ready, and it was dispatched to Smith coupled with the suggestion that with this material in hand he could commence work on the introduction. Here a problem arose in that A.M. Klein's contribution to the anthology had been changed, and Smith expressed strong concern over what he felt was the proposed inclusion of inferior poems. In a long letter of four pages dated 19 February 1934, Smith argued for stronger poetry from Klein ('most important of all is for Klein to put in enough material that is worthy of him'). In addition, Smith said:

> It seems to me the book is going to be somewhat too slim. To remedy this I suggest — (1) We include 'The Titans' as Pratt's contribution (2) We print some poems by Dorothy Livesay (3) You go systematically through the files of the C.F. [*Canadian Forum*] and find some isolated poems of merit — ...

'(1)' he emphasized, 'is quite important.' Scott was some time in answering, but when he did write on 26 March 1934, he informed Smith that:

> We have weighed all your advice most seriously, and this is the result. The selection from Klein has been entirely changed. We are going to include OUT OF THE PULVER AND POLISHED LENS, THE SOIREE OF VELVEL KLEINBURGER and one or two of the short poems that you have agreed upon with Leo [Kennedy].

Of the strong suggestion regarding Pratt's 'The Titans' Scott had this to say:

> Titans is a creditable piece of work, but it is rather rollicking seafaring stuff. It is alright for what it is, but what is it? We prefer the less successful but more experimental and more contemporary work of the poems we have included. It belongs to our Anthology in spirit if not in skill.

There the matter rested, with Scott continuing to steer the manuscript into necessary revisions and a second draft. He put off the suggested inclusion of Dorothy Livesay to a planned second edition of the anthology, and urged Smith on with the work of what was now becoming a languishing introduction. By mid-April, though, Smith had regained his stride, and, with one eye fixed, as it were, on the model supplied by Michael Roberts's *New Signatures* which had appeared two years earlier under the imprint of Leonard and Virginia Woolf at the Hogarth Press in London, he wrestled with the problem of introducing the work of his associates. Few have realized what a striking resemblance *New Provinces* bears, visually and in spirit of conception, to that predecessor. Following the pattern of Roberts's 'Preface,' Smith considered the possibility of writing capsule appraisals of the poetry of each one of the six contributors. He toyed with the idea of turning the Kennedy and Finch sections of the introduction over to either G.W. Latham or S.I. Hayakawa, although Scott squelched this notion resolutely in his letter of 8 May 1934, in which, unwittingly, he may have given faint intimations of trouble to come:

> I don't want to submit the introduction to Toronto until it is
> finished. Leo [Kennedy] tells me Finch and Pratt are a bit
> opposed to the whole idea of one. We had better present them
> with a fait accompli.

For Smith, this was proving to be a difficult year. His opinion about the usefulness of an introduction had shifted somewhat, and now, caught up in the anxious business of securing a permanent academic appointment, he had little patience and less time for the nagging task of preface writing.

On 8 June 1934, things seemed to be coming to a head, darkly, and Scott wrote:

> I have just got back from a trip to New York and Leo [Kennedy] tells me that he had rather serious news from you. I congratulate you on your Chicago job (I suppose you really want it) but your refusal to do any more work on the introduction to the Anthology is a crime of the first magnitude.

Smith responded in mid-June, writing to say that he had a prospect of a job in advertising in Chicago, and that he was going to look things over in that city. Clearly his mind was on things other than slim anthologies of verse and the chores of their introductions. Scott, however, persisted, firm and cajoling, invoking from time to time the yea-saying encouragement of Leo Kennedy. Late in July, Smith had given up on the Chicago prospect and had returned to Canada, and from Magog, Quebec, he dispatched the finished introduction with a gracious salute: 'Here's your goddamn preface.' Things, apparently, were at a low ebb, and there the matter seemed to rest although Scott in his orchestrating role was in for tougher times. The project had lost momentum while Scott cast about for a likely publisher. It was not until September of that year that Pratt began to figure in the negotiations with Hugh Eayrs of the Macmillan Company of Canada, a publisher on whom Scott had long set his mind. They were, of course, Pratt's publishers, and had produced Kennedy's *The Shrouding* in 1933 and would be issuing Collin's collection of essays, *The White Savannahs*. In fact, Scott's experiences in finding a publisher for the anthology had been generally disappointing. Most of the houses which he approached proved uninterested, and even Macmillan was cautious and reserved about the idea. At a loss as to how to make the collection more appealing, Scott had even contemplated changing the proposed title to 'Tangents' in order to break a too obvious and imitative association with the English counterpart anthologies, *New Signatures* and *New Country*.

In October, the work, newly retyped and complete with Smith's preface, finally fell into the hands of Pratt, and therefore under the scrutiny of Robert Finch and Eayrs, upon whom Pratt had been urging the collection. On 7 November 1934, Pratt wrote to Scott outlining the conditions under which Macmillan would consider doing the book. They proposed an associated venture in which the authors would find subscribers for the volume to the tune of two hundred to two hundred and fifty dollars. Almost casually Pratt added:

> Eayrs also objects to the Preface. He says it is unwise, and
> would stir up unneccessary antagonisms. Let the Scott-[D.C.]
> Roberts group alone and let the volume stand on its own feet
> without the initial 'nose-tweaking' as he describes it.

Macmillan's proposal as reported by Pratt, besides appearing high-handed with Smith's preface, struck the group as quite unacceptable. Kennedy urged another publisher; Scott preferred a privately printed edition rather than a joint venture with a commercial house; and there arose, in addition, the problem of paying a permission fee to Macmillan for the use of Pratt's poetry. By the end of the year – December 1934 – things had come to such a pass that Pratt was offering to withdraw from the anthology, and Scott was manoeuvring delicately to keep the undertaking alive. It would be fully a year before the project would regain its momentum, a year during which Scott's energies would be devoted to a crucial election, and it would be 30 October 1935 before he could again address himself to *New Provinces* and to Arthur Smith: 'I have decided something definite must be done about this anthology.' In November, talks with Eayrs had been resumed, and Scott was prepared for a co-adventure in the publication of the anthology, although he continued to have his misgivings. To Pratt — 28 November 1935:

> I hope you will approve of the idea, though it is rather late for us to be bringing out the anthology. It may well be that it will be more suited to the temper of the coming boom years than to the tensions of the economic depression.

At the same time, Smith, caught in an unsatisfactory job, sent off a tired and depressing postcard to Scott from Vermillion, South Dakota. It said, in part:

> ...I don't care for *my* poems in the collection much now (with about 3 exceptions). ... The Preface wd. have to be carefully rewritten — and the whole book is quite out of date.

But early in December 1935, Smith was writing in a happier, more constructive frame of mind. He wanted some changes in his contribution, and planned to revise the preface. In the meantime he warned anxiously: 'For God's sake let the format and everything about the printing of the book and its general makeup be modest and simple.' Smith was buoyed up also by a letter from W.E. Collin, whose *The White Savannahs* was going to be published in April of the following year. It looked as if *New Provinces* would appear at the same time and, as Smith suggested wryly: 'Apparently a new school of young Canadian poets is

going to spring into being on that significant date [1 April 1936].'
On 30 January 1936, it was possible for Scott to write to Smith
announcing that arrangements with Macmillan for the publication
of *New Provinces* were 'fairly complete.' But the second para-
graph of that letter contained a bomb. Scott reported:

> I am afraid the whole of your excellent preface has had to be
> scrapped. Macmillan's I think would have published it, but
> Pratt and Finch put their feet down flat.

This 'putting down of the foot' had taken place — quite unex-
pectedly, one could say — in a letter of Pratt's dated 20 Decem-
ber 1935. Writing on the stationery of the newly founded (but
yet to be published) *Canadian Poetry Magazine* with which he
was then much occupied — especially in rallying writers to the
periodical, and in soliciting material for it — Pratt tucked away
this middle paragraph:

> I went over the ms. and read for proof, then took it over to Finch
> who did likewise. Finch feels very strongly that the Preface
> ought to go. He doesn't like the tone of it and the general im-
> pression which will be left on the public mind that Canadian
> literature had to wait for us to get its first historical success.
> We talked it over with Eayrs who likes the verse but is very
> dubious about the prologue. He calls it 'nose-tweaking.' Per-
> sonally I would feel more contented with a small foreword...

That Scott, weary of the push and pull to which he had been
subjected in the course of two years of trying to manage the
anthology into being, was reconciled to changes in the preface is
evident in his own note of 29 December 1935, addressed to Pratt.
In it he says:

> Perhaps you are right about the Preface for the anthology. I
> am still convinced it is correct in its general accusation...

Smith's reaction to this news, however, was understandably one
of anger and exasperation. He exploded in his own letter to Scott
on 6 February 1936 and annouuced that he wanted nothing to do
with the anthology since 'I don't see how the publication of the
book can perform any useful service to any one whatsoever.'
Within four days, Scott was back to him, once more holding the
line, once more reassuring:

> I have your last letter of open rebellion. All I can say is, please
> do not throw a monkey wrench in the works at this point. ... I
> am so tied up with Macmillan's now that it is practically
> impossible to withdraw. So please wait until you receive the
> page proofs, which I hope will reach you early in March.

Scott then, with the help of Kennedy, prepared a new and greatly
shortened preface to replace the rejected introduction. This was
shown to Smith, who made several small but significant textual
changes, and, in a scribbled footnote, snapped: 'This vague, aim-
less *jargon* (cf. par. 3) is not going to do the book much good.'
March and April 1936 were taken up with putting the anthology
through the machinery at Macmillan. The arrangements, finally,
were that the contributors would put up two hundred dollars
with the publisher, and Scott busied himself rounding up this
money and seeing to the book's design and production. It came
off the presses on 9 May 1936 and was officially published when
fifteen copies were presented to the newspapers on 12 May 1936.
How the anthology fared in terms of sales and public reception is

best told in Scott's own words. Reporting to Pratt a year and a half after publication (2 November 1937) he had this to say:

> I have now something to report as to the sales of NEW
> PROVINCES. From May 9th, 1936 to March 31st, 1937 the
> magnificent number of 82 copies was sold, of which I
> purchased 10. This despite the fact that we have had excellent
> reviews from the only people in this country who may be
> considered serious critics. So I take it that we do not retire to
> a life of poetry and ease.

There are some subtle and painful ironies in what happened to *New Provinces* after its appearance. Macmillan saw to the routine of a proper release to the press, and review copies were duly sent out to the key journals of the time. But the notices or attention which the anthology really received were disappointing. The review in *The Canadian Forum* was a brief omnibus item which included three other collections of verse, one bearing the ludicrous title *East of my House and West of the Water Tank*. The reviewer was Edgar McInnis, assistant professor of history in the University of Toronto who, having called his review — rather ominously, I should think — 'The Disturbed Muse,' went on to praise Pratt in the little space afforded *New Provinces* for 'his vigor, his enthusiasm, his sense of irony allied with the remarkable pictorial quality of his imagination...' *Queen's Quarterly* was greatly taken with the work of British poets in those years, and while the latest work of John Masefield, the poet laureate, was reviewed elaborately, *New Provinces* got short shrift. In *The Dalhousie Review*, *The White Savannahs* and *New Provinces* were considered together with most of the mention going to W.E.

Collin's pioneer work of criticism. Of the critics, E.K. Brown writing in the 'Letters in Canada' supplement of the *University of Toronto Quarterly* proved to be most perceptive and intelligent in his response. He hailed the appearance of the anthology as one of 'three extremely important services [which had] been rendered to Canadian poetry' during 1936. The others were the publication of *The White Savannahs* and the launching of the *Canadian Poetry Magazine*. For Brown, *New Provinces* marked 'the emergence before the general readers of the country ... of a group of poets who may well have as vivifying an effect on Canadian poetry as the Group of Seven had on Canadian printing.' That the general readership failed to respond to this important new collection is amply proven in the gallows humour in which Pratt and Scott indulged in their annual exchange of letters accompanied by minuscule royalty cheques. Perhaps Pratt could have helped the collection along had he arranged for a serious review article in the *Canadian Poetry Magazine*, of which he was editor and which reached a relatively large and interested poetry audience. An impact in that circle would have meant something. But no review appeared.

The recognition of *New Provinces* has been, generally speaking, a belated and distant doffing of critical hats. Desmond Pacey recognized its importance in his essays on A.J.M. Smith and F.R. Scott in *Ten Canadian Poets* (1958); and Munro Beattie called it 'a literary milestone' in his chapter, 'Poetry, 1935-1950' in the *Literary History of Canada* (1965). It is of course true that those who have worked with Canadian writing, the poets and critics and teachers of modern poetry, have all known the importance of this anthology; it is all the more ironic, then, that it has taken us forty years to see this new edition of it into print.

NOTES

1   As quoted by Peter Jones in his introduction to his edition of *Imagist Poetry* (Penguin 1972) 14
2   In his *New Bearings in English Poetry: A Study of the Contemporary Situation* (Penguin in association with Chatto and Windus 1963) 172
3   William York Tindall, *Forces in Modern British Literature 1885-1956* (New York 1956) 48
4   *Ibid.*

Acknowledgements

I am grateful to F.R. Scott for his early interest in this project and his steady encouragement, which included access to his papers. I also wish to thank A.J.M. Smith for his helpful criticism.

Acknowledgement is due to the owners of copyright, Robert Finch, Leo Kennedy, and F.R. Scott, and to the publishers listed below, without whose co-operation this undertaking would not have been realized.

'A Rejected Preface' is reprinted by permission of University of British Columbia Press from A.J.M. Smith, *Towards a View of Canadian Letters: Selected Critical Essays, 1928-1971* (Vancouver: University of British Columbia Press 1973) 170-3.

A.M. Klein's 'Out of the Pulver and the Polished Lens' and 'Soirée of Velvel Kleinburger' are reprinted by permission of McGraw-Hill Ryerson Limited, publishers of *The Collected Poems of A.M. Klein* compiled by Miriam Waddington, Copyright©1974.

E.J. Pratt's 'The Prize Winner' (later entitled 'The Prize Cat'), 'Text of the Oath,' 'The Convict Holocaust,' 'From Java to Geneva' (later entitled 'From Stone to Steel'), 'The Man and the Machine,' 'Seen on the Road,' 'The Drag-Irons,' and 'Sea-Gulls' are reprinted by permission of The Macmillan Company of Canada Limited, publishers of *The Collected Poems of E.J. Pratt* edited by Northrop Frye (Toronto: 2nd ed. 1958).

A.J.M. Smith's 'Shadows There Are,' 'Like an Old Proud King in a Parable,' 'In the Wilderness,' 'The Two Sides of a Drum,' 'Prothalamium,' 'Epitaph,' 'The Creek,' 'The Lonely Land,' 'To a Young Poet,' 'A Soldier's Ghost,' 'News of the Phoenix,' and 'Offices of the First and the Second Hour' are reprinted by permission of Oxford University Press Canada, publishers of *Poems: New and Collected* (Toronto 1967).

A Rejected Preface

The bulk of Canadian verse is romantic in conception and conventional in form. Its two great themes are nature and love — nature humanized, endowed with feeling, and made sentimental; love idealized, sanctified, and inflated. Its characteristic type is the lyric. Its rhythms are definite, mechanically correct, and obvious; its rhymes are commonplace.

The exigencies of rhyme and rhythm are allowed to determine the choice of a word so often that a sensible reader is compelled to conclude that the plain sense of the matter is of only minor importance. It is the arbitrarily chosen verse pattern that counts. One has the uncomfortable feeling in reading such an anthology as W.W. Campbell's *The Oxford Book of Canadian Verse* or J.W. Garvin's *Canadian Poets* that the writers included are not interested in saying anything in particular; they merely wish to show that they are capable of turning out a number of regular stanzas in which statements are made about the writer's emotions, say 'In Winter,' or 'At Montmorenci Falls,' or 'In A Birch Bark Canoe.' Other exercises are concerned with pine trees, the open road, God, snowshoes or Pan. The most popular experience is to be pained, hurt, stabbed or seared by beauty — preferably by the yellow flame of a crocus in the spring or the red flame of a maple leaf in autumn.

There would be less objection to these poems if the observation were accurate and its expression vivid, or if we could feel

*This text of A.J.M. Smith's preface is the one contained in his
Towards a View of Canadian Letters (Vancouver 1973) 170-3.

that the emotion was a genuine and intense one. We could then go on to ask if it were a valuable one. But, with a negligible number of exceptions, the observation is general in these poems and the descriptions are vague. The poet's emotions are un-bounded, and are consequently lacking in the intensity which results from discipline and compression; his thinking is of a trans-cendental or theosophical sort that has to be taken on faith. The fundamental criticism that must be brought against Canadian poetry as a whole is that it ignores the intelligence. And as a result it is dead.

Our grievance, however, against the great dead body of poetry laid out in the mortuary of the *Oxford Book* or interred under Garvin's florid epitaphs is not so much that it is dead but that its sponsors in Canada pretend that it is alive. Yet it should be ob-vious to any person of taste that this poetry cannot now, and in most cases never could, give the impression of being vitally con-cerned with real experience. The Canadian poet, if this kind of thing truly represents his feelings and his thoughts, is a half-baked, hyper-sensitive, poorly adjusted, and frequently neurotic individual that no one in his senses would trust to drive a car or light a furnace. He is the victim of his feelings and fancies, or of what he fancies his feelings ought to be, and his emotional aber-rations are out of all proportion to the experience that brings them into being. He has a soft heart and a soft soul; and a soft head. No wonder nobody respects him, and few show even the most casual interest in his poetry. A few patriotic professors, one or two hack journalist critics, and a handful of earnest antholo-gists — these have tried to put the idea across that there exists a healthy national Canadian poetry which expresses the vigorous hope of this young Dominion in a characteristically Canadian style, but the idea is so demonstrably false that no one but the interested parties has been taken in.

We do not pretend that this volume contains any verse that might not have been written in the United States or in Great Britain. There is certainly nothing specially Canadian about more than one or two poems. Why should there be? Poetry today is written for the most part by people whose emotional and intellectual heritage is not a national one; it is either cosmopolitan or provincial, and for good or evil, the forces of civilization are rapidly making the latter scarce.

A large number of the verses in this book were written at a time when the contributors were inclined to dwell too exclusively on the fact that the chief thing wrong with Canadian poetry was its conventional and insensitive technique. Consequently, we sometimes thought we had produced a good poem when all we had done in reality was not produce a conventional one. In Canada this is a deed of some merit.

In attempting to get rid of the facile word, the stereotyped phrase and the mechanical rhythm, and in seeking, as the poet today must, to combine colloquialism and rhetoric, we were of course only following in the path of the more significant poets in England and the United States. And it led, for a time, to the creation of what, for the sake of brevity, I will call 'pure poetry.'

A theory of pure poetry might be constructed on the assumption that a poem exists as a thing in itself. It is not a copy of anything or an expression of anything, but is an individuality as unique as a flower, an elephant or a man on a flying trapeze. Archibald MacLeish expressed the idea in *Ars Poetica* when he wrote.

A poem should not mean, but be.

Such poetry is objective, impersonal, and in a sense timeless and absolute. It stands by itself, unconcerned with anything save its own existence.

Not unconnected with the disinterested motives that produce pure poetry are those which give rise to imagist poetry. The imagist seeks with perfect objectivity and impersonality to re-create a thing or arrest an experience as precisely and vividly and simply as possible. Kennedy's 'Shore,' Scott's 'Trees in Ice,' my own 'Creek' are examples of the simpler kind of imagist verse; Finch's 'Teacher,' tiny as it is, of the more complex. In 'Shore' and 'Creek' the reader may notice that the development of the poem depends upon metrical devices as much as on images; the music is harsh and the rhythm difficult.

Most of the verses in this book are not, however, so uncon-cerned with thought as those mentioned. In poems like 'Epithalamium,' 'The Five Kine,' 'Words for a Resurrection,' and 'Like An Old Proud King' an attempt has been made to fuse thought and feeling. Such a fusion is characteristic of the kind of poetry usually called metaphysical. Good metaphysical verse is not, it must be understood, concerned with the communication of ideas. It is far removed from didactic poetry. What it is con-cerned with is the emotional effect of ideas that have entered so deeply into the blood as never to be questioned. Such poetry is primarily lyrical; it should seem spontaneous. Something of the quality I am suggesting is to be found in such lines as

The wall was there, oh perilous blade of glass

or

This Man of April walks again.

xxx

In the poems just mentioned thought is the root, but it flowers in the feeling. They are essentially poems of the sensibility, a little bit melancholy, perhaps a little too musical. A healthier robustness is found in satirical verse, such as Scott's much needed counterblast against the Canadian Authors' Association, or in the anti-romanticism of Klein's

And my true love,
She combs and combs,
The lice from off
My children's domes.

The appearance of satire, and also of didactic poetry that does not depend upon wit, would be a healthy sign in Canadian poetry. For it would indicate that our poets are realizing, even if in an elementary way, that poetry is more concerned with expressing exact ideas than wishy-washy 'dreams.' It would indicate, too, that the poet's lofty isolation from events that are of vital significance to everybody was coming to an end.

Detachment, indeed, or self-absorption is (for a time only, I hope) becoming impossible. The era of individual liberty is in eclipse. Capitalism can hardly be expected to survive the cataclysm its most interested adherents are blindly steering towards, and the artist who is concerned with the most intense of experiences must be concerned with the world situation in which, whether he likes it or not, he finds himself. For the moment at least he has something more important to do than to record his private emotions. He must try to perfect a technique that will combine power with simplicity and sympathy with intelligence so that he may play his part in developing mental and emotional attitudes that will facilitate the creation of a more practical social system.

Of poetry such as this, there is here only the faintest fore-shadowing — a fact that is not unconnected with the backward-ness politically and economically of Canada — but that Canadian poetry in the future must become increasingly aware of its duty to take cognizance of what is going on in the world of affairs we are sure.

That the poet is not a dreamer, but a man of sense; that poetry is a discipline because it is an art; and that it is further a useful art: these are propositions which it is intended this volume shall suggest. We are not deceiving ourselves that it has proved them.

New Provinces

Poems of Several Authors

PREFACE

What has been described as the "new poetry" is now a quarter of a century old. Its two main achievements have been a development of new techniques and a widening of poetic interest beyond the narrow range of the late Romantic and early Georgian poets. Equipped with a freer diction and more elastic forms, the modernists sought a content which would more vividly express the world about them.

This search for new content was less successful than had been the search for new techniques, and by the end of the last decade the modernist movement was frustrated for want of direction. In this, poetry was reflecting the aimlessness of its social environment.

In confronting the world with the need to restore order out of social chaos, the economic depression has released human energies by giving them a positive direction. The poet today shares in this release, and contemporary English and American verse as a consequence shows signs of regaining the vitality it had lost.

The poems in this collection were written for the most part when new techniques were on trial, and when the need for a new direction was more apparent then the knowledge of what that direction would be. *New Provinces* contains work which has had significance for the authors in the evolution of their own understanding.

March, 1936

ACKNOWLEDGEMENTS

Acknowledgements are due to the following magazines for the use of poems which have appeared in their pages: *The Canadian Poetry Magazine*, for two poems of Robert Finch; *The Dial, The Rocking Horse, The Canadian Forum*, for poems of Leo Kennedy; *The Menorah Journal*, for poems of A. M. Klein; *The Canadian Forum*, for poems of E. J. Pratt; *The Canadian Mercury, The Canadian Forum*, for poems of F. R. Scott; *The Dial, Hound & Horn, The Nation, Poetry: A Magazine of Verse*, and *New Verse*, for poems of A. J. M. Smith.

CONTENTS

Page

ROBERT FINCH

LEO KENNEDY

A. M. KLEIN

vii

Robert Finch

THE FIVE KINE

Down from the distant pasture of my ease
their lean flanks scarred against the wall of duty
    come the five kine I never sought to please,
come in a famished parody of beauty.
    Their eyes are dim, their udders drop no milk,
their hooves are splayed, their flanks, sunken and sooty,
    augur a dearth of inauspicious ilk.
Barns must be raised and food be found for keeping
    when no expected corn hides in the silk,
but that perpetual harvest none went reaping,
    soil so exuberant was never tilled,
and still the kine kept feeding, feeding and sleeping.
    Pasture of ease, what vigilance withheld
froze the intrepid marrow of your grass?
    The kine were there, fivefold and safely belled,
The wall was there, oh perilous blade of glass,
    sheering denial between pent and wrung,
The soil was there, long, long ago, alas
    so long. The kine too had been there for long,
yet now they seek the faithless drover's goad
    as he the scattered purchase of a song,
while leisure is become a desert road.

EGG-AND-DART

This never-ended searching for the eyes
Wherein the unasked question's answer lies;
This beating, beating, beating of the heart
Because a contour seems to fit the part;
The long, drear moment of the look that spoils
The little bud of hope; the word that soils
The pact immaculate, so newly born;
The noisy silence of the old self-scorn;
These, and the sudden leaving in the lurch;
Then the droll recommencement of the search.

BEAUTY MY FOND FINE CARE

beauty my fond fine care whose wings are clipt
whose cage is shrunk, whose aliment reduced,
juster the note, the counterpoint more apt,
more erudite the company seduced.

circumscribed flight and tailored freedom tame
zealous unequals to a fastidious bound
since but the bars determining our name
from the profane ground mark the holy ground.

beauty my fond fine care, no vaunt collapses
the promise made though sworn perforce in laughter,
memory, beauty, in a unique ellipsis
modulate fact to faith, now, and for after.

WINDOW-PIECE

Trees; hands upthrust in tattered black lace mitts,
enormous brooms stuck handle down in snow,
the nervous roots of giant buried flowers.
Old willows in spun copper periwigs,
and many-fingered firs smoothing white stoles
beside the drained rococo lily-pool
whose shuddering cherub wrings an icicle
from the bronze gullet of his frozen swan.

The hedge, the driveway, mock in counterpoint
the inverted canon of the winding creek
whose little fall boils in a bowl of ice
under the bent back of the patient bridge.
Lacks a blue buck bearing vermilion horns
led by a groom in tightest daffodil?
The silent steam shovel gathers its dark mass
to leap upon the pale red water-tower.

THE HERO

in heaving scarlet
the rustic conqueror
clips his nag
with immaculate leg
bends with a cant

to the overall-conquered,
get up, stoke, stoking,
get up, get up steam,

bends with a cant,
canters, is
gone
                        poppy
that kindles
the dream in a word

get   up

THE HUNT

pale
    purple hill
oh paler far

blue horse
        white hooved
spurn purple mire

bite
    cinnamon leopard
the pale doe's flank

shoot
    red spurred rider
your patient arrow

TEACHER

Examinations snow
between our meeting;
my burning pencil
melts the white hindrance.

BECOME THAT VILLAGE

Become that village where a world
in small prevents my poverty,
a common to community
beyond the seas of access hurled.

In those ungeometric streets
whose light no system may predict,
house me so nothing shall evict
my hope, my hope and its defeats,

which, villeins for their manored lord,
will feed on unmolested game,
asking no honour but his name,
with silence, their exact reward,

silence, before a silent tree
to tabulate the mocking brief
unconscious transit of a leaf,
the curt migration of the bee.

THE HAMMERS

One in the fist
compels a nail
to cover rest
from heat and hail.

And one to music
beats a wire
until the heart
dissolves in fire.

For food or fleece
one speeds a ball,
for ending peace,
or ending all.

And one can make
persuasion fast
to lightning's
iridescent mast.

FROM A HAMMOCK

Policeman of contentment, stay
the official process of dismay,

Arrest each ambush thought has laid,
Nip it in bud, clip it in blade,

Escort these eyes to walk the wood
of sloth, the labyrinth of mood,

through a green algebra to brims
of water where reflection swims,

to where, its spring ordeal sustained,
the willow mourns the trophy gained,

while poplar pedestals, that fling
askew to stretch this cloud of string,

topple the cloud of cloud they bear
to cushions for the patient stare

that holds both vision and the viewed
fixt, in a soundless solitude

whose brilliant exile, for the heart,
is, and not makes, a work of art.

THE EXCURSIONISTS

What muniment a mind must have
Before it stammer I believe,
Maugre the feats it can or may do
Balking incontinent at Credo,
Hating the leap from pro to con
Across the gulf of Erewhon.

Escapeless Odyssey, to go
This distance between yes and no,
To breathe the breath that will transmute
A relative to absolute,
That faith to life's conundrum buy
The unpronounceable reply.

Vertiginous journey through a skull
To banyans of romantic shade
Or classic cemeteries clayed
With function freezing in a lull:
Different though be the destination
One fare is honoured either station,

And whether may if yet or but,
On no, on yes, both gates are shut.

Leo Kennedy

EPITHALAMIUM

This body of my mother, pierced by me
In grim fulfilment of our destiny,
Now dry and quiet as her fallow womb
Is laid beside the shell of that bridegroom
My father, who with eyes towards the wall
Sleeps evenly; his dust stirs not at all
No syllable of greeting curls his lips,
As to that shrunken side his leman slips.

Yet these are two of unabated worth
Who in the shallow bridal bed of earth
Find youth's fecundity, and of their swift
Comminglement of bone and sinew, lift
—A lover's seasonable gift to blood
Made bitter by a parchèd widowhood—
This bloom of tansy from the fertile ground:
My sister, heralded by no moan, no sound.

MOLE TALK

The weasel and the wren consort
   Beneath one coverlet,
Upon the whittled bones of each
   Docility is set;
Strange fellows for a common bed,
   The rodent and the bird
Lip-deep in sand and gravel, lie
   Without a grudging word.
No shuddering disports the worm,
   Too wise are they, and proud,
To lift a stiffened limb, or pluck
   The seaming of a shroud.

PROPHECY FOR ICARUS

No bird that streams its feathers back
And plunges softly out
Through cubic densities of space
Then banks, and climbs aslant,
But will drop fluttering with woe,
And flex its wings, dismayed
To feel time-brittled tendons halt,
And know itself betrayed.

SHORE

Sand shifts with every tide, and gravel
Slurs against the rock,
Weeds and a little lifted silt remain
Marking the reach of water, the long shock
Of an absent tide.
Here is no stencilled track of tern, no trace
Of the slight feet of curlews, here no lace
Of foam for the braided webs of gulls to press
Into the falling bosom of the sea

. . . But silt left by the receded tide, a ravel
Of weeds thrown high by the wash of water, a crest
Of wave, distant, beyond the cove.

LETTER TO GIRLS

Now that the ritual resumes,
And the quick season makes its play,
And surges up the urgent sap,
And tups the dove, and dips the spray

To shudder blossom over rock,
To scatter madness in the blood,
Provoke a tidal from an ebb,
And germinate and plump a bud:

Cup lovers' hands about your breasts,
And give them kisses sharp as wine,
And speed the cycle of your need
With swelling fields and fruitful kine.

DELICATE CLAY

a sculptured head by E. N.

This delicate clay poised fiercely against time
That eats seas and continents, reshapes in molecule
Flesh granite feather and bone and iron
Asserts the furtive anguish of the breed,
The hands upraised, the diffident recoil,
Yet hawklike defies extinction and exults
For breath-drawn seed sown trees wind-shaken.

WORDS FOR A RESURRECTION

Each pale Christ stirring underground
Splits the brown casket of its root,
Wherefrom the rousing soil upthrusts
A narrow, pointed shoot,

And bones long quiet under frost
Rejoice as bells precipitate
The loud ecstatic sundering,
The hour inviolate.

This Man of April walks again—
Such marvel does the time allow—
With laughter in his blessed bones,
And lilies on his brow.

EPITHALAMIUM BEFORE FROST

Now that leaves shudder from the hazel limb,
And poppies pod, and maples whirl their seed,
And squirrels dart from private stores to slim
The oak of acorns with excessive greed;

And now that sap withdraws, and black geese skim
In rigid phalanx over sedge and reed,
And rime surmised at morning pricks the rim
Of tawny stubble, husk and perishing weed—

Now shall I cry Epithalamium!
Over the bed which your two forms have pressed;
And bid earth's fertile spirits stir and come
To winter at your hearth and make it blessed;
Until returns the bridal trillium,
And the first crocus hoists its yellow crest!

A BRIGHT SWAN FOR MY DAUGHTER

Now preen your swan-bright breast, my lovely daughter,
And I shall tell you of Leda's noble lover
Than whom no statelier drifted on blue water.

This lady took such joy no mouth may utter
To bid his feathered lust rape all her treasure,
And in his fierce embrace sweetly to shudder,

Till from that surging loin in wondrous measure
The play of stinging barbs did so distraught her
That cried upon the slanting air her pleasure

To shape within her flesh a noble daughter
For whose swan breast sighed many a stately lover,
And towers scorched black and ships veered over water.

TESTAMENT

Old fathers arrogant and stern, the chalk
pressed tight against your temples, the live root
slurring the moist stained bone as seasons further
the issue of your loins to later spasm;

ancients placid under turf, dulled to the movement
of seed swelling, sprout lifting, rain slithering over
the gnarled husk, the fiercely crowding humus;

bearded ones at ease with your passion, dust with your
                              fathers' fathers and your sons' sons;
ancestors remembered though not known, proudly aloof
from time and weeping, quick again in me and my children;

progenitors walking the pavement with me, observing sumach
in the close Ontario woods, thinking in a new country
that breath is breath anywhere,
that sweat is good and women generous to lie with,
that sons grow tall and disregard example—

There was John a baler on Birkenhead docks,
and Walter the strong teamster who sang chanties
learned of his father the whaler in '73,
whose father pressed cider in the apple country;
and Peter the master-moulder with his own shop
who hated England and remembered the Rebellion;
and old John Kennedy the smith from Leith
whom Kerry Meg endowed with three brass farthings.

Old fathers angular in death these generations,
whose thews have changed to salts and mixed with gravel,
whose faces blur in mine, whose stiffened tongues

confound with others turning a looser speech—

to you I leave my life which is over and done as you are;
to my sons' children your gift to me, the life unravelled
and which transmutes as time turns, to your portion.

These under my hand in the fall of '34,
these with the breath of life in my body and the blood
prompt at the wrist, the eye alert, the wit
sharpened by past want.

A. M. Klein

OUT OF THE PULVER AND THE POLISHED LENS

I

The paunchy sons of Abraham
Spit on the maculate streets of Amsterdam,
Showing Spinoza, Baruch alias Benedict,
He and his God are under interdict.

Ah, what theology there is in spatted spittle,
And in anathema what sacred prose
Winnowing the fact from the suppose!
Indeed, what better than these two things can whittle
The scabrous heresies of Yahweh's foes,
Informing the breast where Satan gloats and crows,
That saving it leave false doctrine, jot and tittle,
No vigilant thumb will leave its orthodox nose?
What better than ram's horn blown,
And candles blown out by maledictory breath,
Can bring the wanderer back to his very own,
The infidel to his faith?

Nothing, unless it be that from the ghetto
A soldier of God advance to teach the creed,
Using as rod the irrefutable stiletto.

II

Uriel da Costa
Flightily ranted
Heresies one day,
Next day recanted.

Rabbi and bishop
Each vied to smuggle
Soul of da Costa
Out of its struggle.

Confessional hears his
Glib paternoster;
Synagogue sees his
Penitent posture.

What is the end of
This catchechism?
Bullet brings dogma
That suffers no schism.

III

Malevolent scorpions befoul thy chambers,
O my heart; they scurry across its floors,
Leaving the slimy vestiges of doubt.

Banish memento of the vermin; let
No scripture on the wall affright you; no
Ghost of da Costa, no, nor any threat.
Ignore, O Heart, even as didst ignore
The bribe of florins jingling in the purse.

IV

Jehovah is factotum of the rabbis,
And Christ endures diurnal Calvary,
Polyglot God is exiled to the churches;
Synods tell God to be or not to be.

The Lord within his vacuum of heaven
Discourses his domestic policies,
With angels who break off their loud hosannas
To help him phrase infallible decrees.

Soul of Spinoza, Baruch Spinoza bids you
Forsake the god suspended in mid-air,
Seek you that other Law, and leave Jehovah
Play his game of celestial solitaire.

V

Reducing providence to theorems, the horrible atheist compiled
such lore that proved, like proving two and two make four,
that in the crown of God we all are gems. From glass and dust
of glass he brought to light, out of the pulver and the polished
lens, the prism and the flying mote, and hence the infinitesimal
and infinite.

    Is it a marvel, then, that he forsook the abracadabra of the
synagogue, and holding with timelessness a duologue, deciphered
a new scripture in the book? Is it a marvel that he left old
fraud for passion intellectual of god?

VI

Unto the crown of bone cry Suzerain!
Do genuflect before the jewelled brain!

Lavish the homage of the vassal; let
The blood grow heady with strong epithet;

A cirque of the Cabbalist! O proud skull!
O alchemy, O crucible!

Sanctum sanctorum, grottoed hermitage
Where sits the bearded sage!

O golden bowl of Koheleth! and of fate
O hour-glass within the pate!

Circling, O planet in the occiput!
O microcosm, sinew-shut!

Yea, and having uttered this loud Te Deum
Ye have been singularly dumb.

VII

I am weak before the wind; before the sun
    I faint; I lose my strength;
I am utterly vanquished by a star;
    I go to my knees, at length.
Before the song of a bird, before
    The breath of spring or fall
I am lost; before these miracles
    I am nothing at all.

VIII

Lord, accept my hallelujahs; look not askance at these my petty words; unto perfection a fragment makes its prayer.

For thou art the world, and I am part thereof; thou art the blossom and I its fluttering petal . . .

I behold thee in all things, and in all things; Lo, it is myself; I look into the pupil of thine eye, and it is my very countenance I see.

Thy glory fills the earth; it is the earth; the noise of the deep, the moving of many waters, is it not thy voice aloud, O Lord, aloud that all may hear?

The wind through the almond-trees spreads the fragrance of thy robes; the turtle-dove twittering utters diminutives of thy love; at the rising of the sun I behold thy countenance.

32

Yea, and in the crescent moon, thy little finger's finger nail.

If I ascend up into heaven, thou art there; if I make my bed in hell, behold thou art there.

Thou art everywhere; a pillar to thy sanctuary is every blade of grass.

Wherefore I said to the wicked, Go to the ant, thou sluggard, seek thou an audience with God.

On the swift wings of a star, even on the numb legs of a snail, thou dost move, O Lord.

A babe in swaddling clothes laughs at the sunbeams on the door's lintel; the sucklings play with thee; with thee Kopernik holds communion through a lens.

I am thy son, O Lord, and brother to all that lives am I.

The flowers of the field they are kith and kin to me; the lily my sister, the rose is my blood and flesh.

Even as the stars in the firmament move, so does my inward heart, and even as the moon draws the tides in the bay, so does it the blood in my veins.

For thou art the world, and I am part thereof; he who does violence to me, verily sins against the light of day; he is made a deicide.

Howbeit, even in dust I am resurrected, and even in decay I live again.

IX

Think of Spinoza, then, not as you think
Of Shabbathai Zvi who for a time of life
Took to himself the Torah for a wife,
And underneath the silken canopy
Made public: Thou art hallowed unto me.

Think of Spinoza, rather, plucking tulips
Within the garden of Mynherr, forgetting

Dutchmen and Rabbins, and consumptive fretting,
Plucking his tulips in the Holland sun,
Remembering the thought of the Adored,
Spinoza, gathering flowers for the One,
The ever-unwedded lover of the Lord.

SOIRÉE OF VELVEL KLEINBURGER

In back-room dens of delicatessen stores,
In curtained parlours of garrulous barber-shops,
While the rest of the world most comfortably snores
On mattresses, or on more fleshly props,
My brother Velvel vigils in the night,
Not as he did last night with two French whores,
But with a deck of cards that once were white.

He sees three wan ghosts, as the thick smoke fades
Dealing him clubs, and diamonds, hearts and spades.

His fingers, pricked with a tailor's needle, draw
The well-thumbed cards; while Hope weighs down his jaw.

O for the ten spade in its proper place,
    Followed by knave in linen lace,
        The queen with her gaunt face,
            The king and mace,
                The ace!

Then Velvel adds a foot-note to his hoax:
I will not have your wherefores and your buts;
For I am for the Joker and his jokes;
I laugh at your alases and tut-tuts,
My days, they vanish into circular smokes,
My life lies on a tray of cigarette-butts.

For it is easy to send pulpit wind
From bellies sumptuously lined;
Easy to praise the sleep of the righteous, when
The righteous sleep on cushions ten,
And having risen from a well-fed wife
Easy it is to give advice on life.

35

But you who upon sated palates clack a moral,
And pick a sermon from between your teeth,
Tell me with what bay, tell me with what laurel
Shall I entwine the heaven-praising wreath,
I, with whom Deity sets out to quarrel?

But, prithee, wherefore these thumbed cards?

O do not make a pack of cards your thesis
And frame no lesson on a house of cards
Where diamonds go lustreless, and hearts go broken
And clubs do batter the skull to little shards,
And where, because the spade is trump
One must perforce kiss Satan's rump.

For I have heard these things from teachers
With dirty beards and hungry features.

Now, after days in dusty factories,
Among machines that manufacture madness
I have no stomach for these subtleties
About rewards and everlasting gladness;
And having met your over-rated dawns,
Together with milkmen watering their milk,
And having trickled sweat, according to a scale of wages,
Sewing buttons to warm the navels of your business sages,
I have brought home at dusk,
My several bones, my much-flailed husk.

> My meals are grand,
> When supper comes
> I feed on canned
> Aquariums.

The salmon dies.
The evening waits
As I catch flies
From unwashed plates.

And my true love,
She combs and combs,
The lice from off
My children's domes . . .

Such is the idyll of my life.
But I will yet achieve
An easier living and less scrawny wife
And not forever will the foreman have
The aces up his sleeve,
But some day I will place the lucky bet.
(Ho! Ho! the social revolutions on a table of roulette!)

Alas, that Velvel's sigh makes eddies in the smoke.
For what's the use?
While the pale faces grin, his brow is hot;
He grasps a deuce . . .

A nicotined hand beyond the smoke sweeps off the pot.

O good my brother, should one come to you
And knock upon the door at mid of night
And show you, writ in scripture, black on white,
That this is no way for a man to do?—
What a pale laughter from these ghosts, and "Who
Are you, my saint, to show us what is right?

Make a fifth hand, and we will be contrite;
Shuffle the cards, be sociable, Reb. Jew."

My brother's gesture snaps; *I spoke.*
His cheeks seek refuge in his mouth.
His nostrils puff superior smoke.
His lips are brown with drouth.

    Hum a hymn of sixpence,
    A tableful of cards
    Fingers slowly shuffling
    Ambiguous rewards.
    When the deck is opened
    The pauper once more gave
    His foes the kings and aces
    And took himself the knave.

Once more he cuts the cards, and dreams his dream;
A Rolls-Royce hums within his brain;
Before it stands a chauffeur, tipping his hat,
"You say that it will rain, Sir; it will rain!"
Upon his fingers diamonds gleam,
His wife wears gowns of ultra-Paris fashion,
And she boasts jewels as large as wondrous eyes
The eyes of Og, the giant-king of Bashan.

So Velvel dreams; dreaming, he rises, and
Buttons his coat, coughs in his raised lapel,
Gropes his way home; he rings a raucous bell.

E. J. Pratt

THE PRIZE WINNER

Pure blood domestic, guaranteed,
Soft-mannered, musical in purr,
The ribbon had declared the breed,
Gentility was in the fur.

Such feline culture in the gads
No anger ever arched her back—
What distance since those velvet pads
Departed from the leopard's track.

And when I mused how Time had thinned
The jungle strains within the cells,
How human hands had disciplined
These prowling optic parallels,

I saw the generations pass
Along the reflex of a spring,
A bird had rustled in the grass,
The tab had caught it on the wing:

Behind the leap so furtive-wild
Was such ignition in the gleam,
I thought an Abyssinian child
Had cried out in the whitethroat's scream.

TEXT OF THE OATH

Upon what Bible will you swear?
Before whose altar lift your hand?
When kettle-drum and trumpet-blare
Attest you at the witness-stand?

There was another lad I knew,
Blue-eyed and trustful and as mild,
A life-enthusiast like you,
Who scarcely had outgrown the child.

There was a virus in the air
That put the toxin in his blood,
Bugles were blowing everywhere
Breathing romance on sleet and mud.

He wrote his lesson on a slate,
Composed of foreign names to spell—
These to defend and these to hate,
And at the barracks learned it well.

They pinned a medal on his breast
Behind the lines one afternoon:
He had from a machine-gun nest
Annihilated a platoon.

THE CONVICT HOLOCAUST
(*Columbus, Ohio, 1930*)

Waiting their turn to be identified,
After their fiery contact with the walls,
Three hundred pariahs ranged side by side
Upon the floors along the cattle stalls!

The fires consumed their numbers with their breath,
Charred out their names; though many of the dead
Gave proof of valour, just before their death,
That Caesar's legions might have coveted.

But these, still subject to the law's commands,
Received the last insignia of the cell:
The guards went through them, straightened out their hands,
And with the ink-brush got the thumb-prints well.

FROM JAVA TO GENEVA

From stone to bronze, from bronze to steel
Along the road-dust of the sun,
Two revolutions of the wheel
From Java to Geneva run.

The snarl Neanderthal is worn
Close to the smiling Aryan lips,
The civil polish of the horn
Gleams from our praying finger tips.

The evolution of desire
Has but matured a toxic wine,
Drunk long before its heady fire
Reddened Euphrates or the Rhine.

Between the temple and the cave
The boundary lies tissue-thin:
The yearlings still the altars crave
As satisfaction for a sin.

The road goes up, the road goes down—
Let Java or Geneva be—
But whether to the cross or crown
The path lies through Gethsemane.

THE MAN AND THE MACHINE

By right of fires that smelted ore
Which he had tended years before,
The man whose hands were on the wheel
Could trace his kinship through her steel,
Between his body warped and bent
In every bone and ligament,
And this "eight-cylinder" stream-lined,
The finest model yet designed.
He felt his lesioned pulses strum
Against the rhythm of her hum,
And found his nerves and sinews knot
With sharper spasm as she climbed
The steeper grades, so neatly timed
From petrol tank to piston shot—
This creature with the panther grace,
This man with slag upon his face.

SEEN ON THE ROAD

The pundit lectured that the world was young
As ever, frisking like a springtime colt
Around the sun, his mother. The class hung
Upon his words. I listened like a dolt

And muttered that I saw the wastrel drawn
Along the road with many a pitch and bump
By spavined mules—this very day at dawn!
And heading for an ammunition dump.

The savant claimed I heckled him. But—Hell!
I saw the fellow in a tumbril there,
Tattered and planet-wise and far from well,
With Winter roosting in his Alpine hair.

THE DRAG-IRONS

He who had learned for thirty years to ride
The seas and storms in punt and skiff and brig,
Would hardly scorn to take before he died
His final lap in Neptune's whirligig.

But with his Captain's blood he did resent,
With livid silence and with glassy look,
This fishy treatment when his years were spent—
To come up dead upon a grapnel hook.

SEA-GULLS

For one carved instant as they flew,
The language had no simile—
Silver, crystal, ivory
Were tarnished. Etched upon the horizon blue
The frieze must go unchallenged, for the lift
And carriage of the winds would stain the drift
Of stars against a tropic indigo
Or dull the parable of snow.

Now settling one by one
Within green hollows or where curled
Crests caught the spectrum from the sun,
A thousand wings are furled.
No clay-born lilies of the world
Could blow as free
As those wild orchids of the sea.

F. R. Scott

trees in ice

these gaunt prongs and points of trees
pierce the zero air with flame
lean fingers of black ice
steal the sun's drawn fire
to make a burning of a barren bush

underneath
            from
                still
flakes   branch
        of   and
            light   arm
fleck-   fall
    ing   fall
        the
            dark
                white
                    snow

this cruelty is a formal loveliness
on a tree's torn limbs
this glittering pain

MARCH FIELD

Now the old folded snow
Shrinks from black earth.
Now is thrust forth
Heavy and still
The field's dark furrow.

Not yet the flowing
The mound-stirring
Not yet the inevitable flow.
There is a warm wind, stealing
From blunt brown hills, loosening
Sod and cold loam
Round rigid root and stem.

But no seed stirs
In this bare prison
Under the hollow sky.
The stone is not yet rolled away
Nor the body risen.

SURFACES

This rock-borne river, ever flowing
Obedient to the ineluctable laws,
Brings a reminder from the barren north
Of the eternal lifeless processes.
There is an argument that will prevail
In this calm stretch of current, slowly drawn
Toward its final equilibrium.

Come, flaunt the brief prerogative of life,
Dip your small civilized foot in this cold water
And ripple, for a moment, the smooth surface of time.

CALVARY

Where crag and loose stone
stand bare to wind and sky
there come armed men. Steel
clangs upon rock, and bone
breaks under nail. They drag
him here to die, whose frail
young body, being human,
born of a man and a woman,
lies so easy to wound.
The tree is planted in ground
barren and dry, and a creed
roots in the cruel mound.

So, with the body broken,
blood becomes token:
eras are stricken.

THE CANADIAN AUTHORS MEET

Expansive puppets percolate self-unction
Beneath a portrait of the Prince of Wales.
Miss Crotchet's muse has somehow failed to function,
Yet she's a poetess. Beaming, she sails

From group to chattering group, with such a dear
Victorian saintliness, as is her fashion,
Greeting the other unknowns with a cheer—
Virgins of sixty who still write of passion.

The air is heavy with Canadian topics,
And Carman, Lampman, Roberts, Campbell, Scott,
Are measured for their faith and philanthropics,
Their zeal for God and King, their earnest thought.

The cakes are sweet, but sweeter is the feeling
That one is mixing with the *literati*;
It warms the old, and melts the most congealing.
Really, it is a most delightful party.

Shall we go round the mulberry bush, or shall
We gather at the river, or shall we
Appoint a poet laureate this Fall,
Or shall we have another cup of tea?

O Canada, O Canada, Oh, can
A day go by without new authors springing
To paint the native lily, and to plan
More ways to set the selfsame welkin ringing?

TELEOLOGICAL

Note, please, the embryo.
                              Unseeing
It swims into being.
Elan vital,
Thyroid, gonads *et al.,*
Preserve the unities.
Though endless opportunities
Offer, arm joins shoulder.
Ego forms. It grows bolder,
Meets fellow anthropoids
In cell-groups. Avoids
Behaviour that's odd—
Like questioning God,
Not playing games, writing tales,
Or being natural with females.
Leaves home. Gets ambitions.
Works hard in positions.
Takes to golf. Makes contacts.
Drops theories for facts.
Always fills in cheque-stubs.
Becomes president of clubs.
Creates a ripple, disturbs particles.
Manufactures articles.
Occupies a front pew
In *Who's Who.*
The Oxford Group
Knocks him for a loop.
At death the estate
Is admittedly great.
Friends knock off work for hours
To see the funeral and flowers.

Who, who shall deny it a name,
Or cry shame
When it makes the discovery
Of the ovary?
Who can prove the illusion
Against the glow of fusion?

vagrant

he fled beyond the outer star
to spaces where no systems are

beyond the last accepted norm
the final vestiges of form

the compass of his mind   astute
to find a polar absolute
patrolled a mute circumference

the present seemed the only tense

there was no downwards for his feet
even his lust was obsolete

and he   the last dot in the sky
did but accentuate an i

infinity became his own
himself the sole criterion

now you may see him   virginal
content to live in montreal

SUMMER CAMP

Here is a lovely little camp
Built among the Laurentian hills
By a Children's Welfare Society,
Which is entirely supported by voluntary contributions.
All summer long underprivileged children scamper about,
And it is astonishing how soon they look healthy and well.
Two weeks here in the sun and air
Through the kindness of our wealthy citizens
Will be a wonderful help to the little tots
When they return for a winter in the slums.

EFFICIENCY

The efficiency of the capitalist system
Is rightly admired by important people.
Our huge steel mills
Operating at 25 per cent. of capacity
Are the last word in organization.
The new grain elevators
Stored with superfluous wheat
Can load a grain boat in two hours.
Marvellous card-sorting machines
Make it easy to keep track of the unemployed.
There isn't one unnecessary employee
In these textile plants
That require a 75 per cent. tariff protection.
And when our closed shoe-factories re-open
They will produce more footwear than we can possibly buy.
So don't let us start experimenting with socialism
Which everyone knows means inefficiency and waste.

OVERTURE

In the dark room, under a cone of light,
You precisely play the Mozart sonata. The bright
Clear notes fly like sparks through the air
And trace a flickering pattern of music there.

Your hands dart in the light, your fingers flow—
They are ten careful operatives in a row
That pick their packets of sound from steel bars,
Constructing harmonies as sharp as stars.

But how shall I hear old music? This is an hour
Of new beginnings, concepts warring for power,
Decay of systems—the tissue of art is torn
With overtures of an era being born.

And this perfection which is less yourself
Than Mozart, seems a trinket on a shelf,
A pretty octave played before a window
Beyond whose curtain grows a world crescendo.

A. J. M. Smith

SHADOWS THERE ARE

Shadows there are, but shadows such as these
Are shadows only in the mortal mind,
Blown by the spirit, or the spirit's wind.

Yet shadows I have seen, of me deemed deeper,
That backed on nothing in the horrid air,

And try as try, I cannot limn the form
That some of them assume where I shall pass.
They grow transparent, and as sharp, as glass.

LIKE AN OLD PROUD KING IN A PARABLE

A bitter king in anger to be gone
From fawning courtier and doting queen
Flung hollow sceptre and gilt crown away,
And breaking bound of all his counties green
He made a meadow in the northern stone
And breathed a palace of inviolable air
To cage a heart that carolled like a swan,
And slept alone, immaculate and gay,
With only his Pride for a paramour.

O who is that bitter king? It is not I.

Let me, I beseech thee, Father, die
From this fat royal life, and lie
As naked as a bridgroom by his bride,
And let that girl be the cold goddess Pride:

And I will sing to the barren rock
Your difficult, lonely music, heart,
Like an old proud king in a parable.

IN THE WILDERNESS

He walks alone, uncomforted,
In Spring's green ripple, Autumn's red.

Birds, like dark starlight,
Twinkle in the sky, are light

As feathers blown about in a gale,
And their song is as cold and sharp as hail.

The lonely air and the hard ground
Are crying to him with no sound

Words that the hurdy-gurdy year
Whines ceaselessly in his sad ear.

He walks between the green leaf and the red
Like one who follows a beloved dead,

And with a young, pedantic eye
Observes how still the dead do lie.

His gaze is stopped in the hard earth
And cannot penetrate to heaven's mirth.

THE TWO SIDES OF A DRUM

When Night lets down her hair
Over the pale blossom
Of the world, far, far from here
With sealed eyes, still bosom
And folded feet I fare
To that country under dream
Where eternity and time are
The two sides of a drum.

PROTHALAMIUM

Here in this narrow room there is no light;
The dead tree sings against the window pane;
Sand shifts a little, easily; the wall
Responds a little, inchmeal, slowly, down.
My sister, whom my dust shall marry, sleeps
Alone, yet knows what bitter root it is
That stirs within her: see, it splits the heart—
Warm hands grown cold, grown nerveless, as a fin ,
And lips enamelled to a hardness—
Consummation ushered in
By wind in sundry corners.

This holy sacrament was solemnized
In harsh poetics a good while ago—
At Malfi and the Danish battlements,
And by that preacher from a cloud in Paul's.
No matter: each must read the truth himself,
Or, reading it, reads nothing to the point.
Now these are me, whose thought is mine, and hers,
Who are alone here in this narrow room—
Tree fumbling pane, bell tolling,
Ceiling dripping and the plaster falling,
And Death, the voluptuous, calling.

EPITAPH

Weep not on this quiet stone:
I, embedded here
Where sturdy roots divide the bone
And tendrils split a hair,
Bespeak you comfort of the grass
That is embodied Me,
Which as I am, not as I was,
Would choose to be.

THE CREEK

Stones
still wet with cold black earth,
roots, whips of roots
and wisps of straw,
green soaked crushed leaves
mud-soiled where hoof has touched them,
twisted grass
and hairs of herbs
that lip the ledge of the stream's edge:

these

then foam-froth, waterweed,
and windblown bits of straw
that rise, subside, float wide,
come round again, subside,
a little changed
and stranger, nearer
nothing:

these

THE LONELY LAND

Cedar and jagged fir
uplift sharp barbs
against the gray
and cloud-piled sky;
and in the bay
blown spume and windrift
and thin, bitter spray
snap
at the whirling sky;
and the pine trees
lean one way.

A wild duck calls
to her mate,
and the ragged
and passionate tones
stagger and fall,
and recover,
and stagger and fall,
on these stones—
are lost
in the lapping of water
on smooth, flat stones.

This is a beauty
of dissonance,
this resonance
of stony strand,
this smoky cry
curled over a black pine
like a broken
and wind-battered branch

when the wind
bends the tips of the pines
and curdles the sky
from the north.

This is the beauty
of strength
broken by strength,
and still strong.

TO A YOUNG POET
for C. A. M.

Tread the metallic nave
Of this windless day with
A pace designed and grave:
Iphigenia in her myth

Creating for stony eyes
An elegant, fatal dance
Was signed with no device
More alien to romance

Than I would have you find
In the stern, autumnal face
Of Artemis, whose kind
Cruelty makes duty grace,

Whose votary alone
Seals the affrighted air
With the worth of a hard thing done
Perfectly, as though without care.

A SOLDIER'S GHOST

How shall I speak
To the regiment of young
Whose throats break
Saluting the god?

Bones
Distilled in the frontier sand
Fumble
The natty chevron.

Can a memberless ghost
Tell?
These lost
Are so many brother bones.

The hieroglyph
Of ash
Concedes an anagram
Of love.

NEWS OF THE PHOENIX

They say the Phoenix is dying, some say dead—
Dead without issue is what one message said,
But that was soon suppressed, officially denied;

I think myself the man who sent it lied,
But the authorities were right to have him shot,
As a precautionary measure, whether he did or not.

THE OFFICES OF THE FIRST AND THE SECOND HOUR

What is the office of the first hour?

TO ABJURE

To abjure the kindness of darkness, humbly
To concede the irrelevant spite of the spirit,
The night-like melancholy flesh-case, and the
Romantic unnecessary cape of the naked heart.

Is the rude root and manlike shape
Of articulate mandrake still godlike in this light?

NAY, WE HAVE GIVEN

Nay, we have given our flesh to the mouth and our
Hearts to the fingers of oblivion. The darkness
Is drained out of us slowly, and these are no more
To us.

What is the office of the second hour?

QUIETLY TO ATTEND

Quietly to attend the unfolding light's stark
Patience, inhuman and faithful like a weed or a flower,
Empty of darkness and light.

LITERATURE OF CANADA

Poetry and Prose in Reprint
Douglas Lochhead, General Editor